T0208595

American Dog House

How to Get In, How to Get Out

Willie GetOut?

IUNIVERSE, INC.
NEW YORK   BLOOMINGTON

American Dog House
How to Get In, How to Get Out

Copyright © 2009 by John Scolaro

All rights reserved. No part of this book may be used or reproduced by any means, graphic, electronic, or mechanical, including photocopying, recording, taping or by any information storage retrieval system without the written permission of the publisher except in the case of brief quotations embodied in critical articles and reviews.

The views expressed in this work are solely those of the author and do not necessarily reflect the views of the publisher, and the publisher hereby disclaims any responsibility for them.

iUniverse books may be ordered through booksellers or by contacting:

iUniverse
1663 Liberty Drive
Bloomington, IN 47403
www.iuniverse.com
1-800-Authors (1-800-288-4677)

Because of the dynamic nature of the Internet, any Web addresses or links contained in this book may have changed since publication and may no longer be valid.

ISBN: 978-1-4401-4898-9 (sc)
ISBN: 978-1-4401-4900-9 (dj)
ISBN: 978-1-4401-4899-6 (ebk)

Printed in the United States of America

iUniverse rev. date: 5/26/2009

Contents

Acknowledgments

I would be remiss if I did not thank Alvaro Maury, Gustavo Morales, David Romano, and Ted Ferrer, members of our gourmet club, for their inspiration and wonderful sense of humor. I would also like to thank John Wrzos, a former security guard at Valencia Community College's West Campus and graduate of Rollins College in Orlando, who suggested the pen name I have assumed as the author of this book. His creativity is obvious.

My wife, Anna, also deserves special recognition for her skillful maneuvers in sending me into the American Dog House more times than I care to remember. Had it not been for her compassion, I would still be in the Dog House today without any hope of getting out.

I am also indebted to my friends Peg Edmonds, Sheryl Kurland, and Paul Licata, and my wife, Anna, who took the time to proofread my book and offer their suggestions. This also includes the exceptional work of my illustrator, Rob Smith Jr. His Web site at www.robsmithjr.com is like a breath of fresh air. My friend and writer Linda Shrieves wrote the excellent preface, which I deeply appreciate. My son, John, deserves a standing ovation for his support of my work from its inception as well as his expertise in making important contacts on my behalf. I will be forever in his debt! Also, the exceptional expertise and availability of Sandee Williams, Training Support Specialist at Valencia Community College's Learning Technology Center/West Campus, is greatly appreciated. Her technical skills and cordial manner are very impressive. This also applies to Maureen Ramsey, former Manager of Valencia's Learning Technology Center/West Campus, and to Alex Nagy, former Senior Instructional Assistant/ Communications Lab/West Campus.

Finally, this book would not have been possible without the influence of Dave Barry, formerly of the *Miami Herald*, and Andy Rooney of CBS's *60 Minutes*. Their uncanny sarcasm, humor, wit, satire, and creativity have impressed me over the years. They see the true nature of reality beyond its literal form.

introduction

It all began in Orlando, Florida, in 1998 with the monthly gourmet club my wife and I started. The club included four married couples we had known since our marriage in 1995. Every month, each couple hosted a special dinner in their own home. These dinners always included humorous exchanges among us men about our experiences in the American Dog House, which was our term for the misery men often create with the women they love. Ask me, I know! In fact, the title of this book derived from such male-only conversations. I told my male counterparts then that I would eventually write a book about our experiences. And, at last, here it is.

My career over the past twenty years as a professor of humanities at Valencia Community College's West Campus has been driven by two passions: teaching and writing. I love to write as much as I love to teach. The experiences I have had as a frequent occupant of the American Dog House and the advice mirrored in this book may help men everywhere avoid such a fate. Humor may be the best medicine after all!

This book is not about me or my close male friends. It is about men everywhere, except those who call Intercourse, Pennsylvania, home. At one time or another, every man has found himself, through no fault of his own, in what Americans call the "Dog House" (or "Dawg House," if you're from the Deep South).

The reason I decided to capitalize the "d" in dog and the "h" in house is simple. The Dog House is an American institution. In fact, it is as American as apple pie. I do not know who invented the phrase "Dog House," or even the exact date of its origin. Maybe this was where Adam was sent by Eve when he imprudently agreed to take a bite of the apple. I suspect that Native American women may have introduced the term when their braves (young or older married males) refused to help around their tepees, preferring instead to "go a-hunting" for two weeks at a click, leaving their women behind to work the fields and clean up after them.

If you don't believe this explanation on the origin of the "Dog House," and I wouldn't blame you if you didn't, then maybe you should blame its origin on your mother's mother (your father's mother would have never done this to you), or better yet, on your mother-in-law. You could even fault Blondie of comics fame for this, since Dagwood—if you believe his creator, Dean Young—has never been able to extricate himself from such a horrific fate. In fact, Dagwood is probably the oldest living occupant of the American Dog House.

Does Dagwood, or any man for that matter, truly deserve such a fate? How do men get into the Dog House anyway? And how can they get out? Is there a Global Dog House? Is there a Dog House for women? Should every man require his wife-to-be to sign a prenuptial agreement with a "No Dog House" clause? Is there a need for a crash course on the American Dog House? What about sex in the American Dog House?

All men everywhere must seek to answer these fundamental questions before they are thrown headlong into the American Dog House. If they default on this assignment, they may be doomed by their wives or partners to spend most of their waking hours in the American Dog House, the likes of which they may hope never to experience again. However, if the inevitable happens and they are unable to avoid such a dismal fate, may God Almighty have mercy on their souls! They may not have another chance to escape, even if they are successful at navigating the questions I have posed above. The American Dog House is waiting for you! Are you ready?

Preface

I first met John Scolaro nearly twenty years ago, when my husband returned to college and had the good luck to land in Scolaro's humanities classroom. Their friendship developed out of a mutual respect for learning and a shared sense of humor.

Over the past decade, I've watched as John created a curriculum of classic literature and humanities for the poor and homeless, with the vision of introducing everyone, regardless of class or income, to the great thinkers.

So it may seem odd that a scholarly man would publish a book about the relationship between husbands and wives—one in which he focuses on men's hapless and hopeless attempts to stay out of what he calls the Dog House.

In this book, John brings a unique perspective and sense of humor to his work. This is a new look at an old subject—viewed through a funhouse mirror.

Linda Shrieves Beaty

How to Get in

Getting into the American Dog House, for most men, is a lot easier than getting out. The men I know are experts at gaining entry. Here is what men usually do or say that nets them a one-way ticket into the American Dog House:

- They vow never to forget their anniversary or the birthday of their wives or partners, but inevitably do.
- They promise to do their share of domestic work when, in fact, they never fulfill such a promise.

- They swear that they will never go out with the boys again to a strip club on a weekend night because they would rather spend the time with their wives or partners, but they go out anyway.

- They say that the woman's voice their wife or partner heard on the phone the other night asking for their husband or partner was just some drunken slut they had been introduced to by a friend of theirs at a conference last year.

- They insist that not including their wives' or partners' mothers in an invitation for Christmas dinner was a gross oversight.

- They vow to pick up their clothes and hang them properly in the closet but end up leaving them on the floor where they innocently threw them in the first place.

- They explain that the XXX-rated photos viewed on the Internet when their wife or partner was out with a girlfriend for coffee was the result of a wrong click of the mouse.

Men honestly believe that the promises they make will be accepted by the women they love. They do not understand that they are actually digging their own graves and are about to cross a new threshold. Here is how this works:

Principles of the American Dog House

1. Use voice inflection as a way of faking genuineness: the higher the pitch, the more serious women think you are!

2. Deny the connections you have established with other women, even if such connections are frivolous and of no consequence.

3. Look and sound as sorry, pathetic, and regretful as you possibly can. This is based on the fact that women are visual and auditory learners.

4. Never show up at the door with a rose or two, much less with a dozen or more, because women will smell a rat every time. Besides, roses are too expensive even under the best conditions, and they die within twenty-four hours.

Have you ever wondered who taught men to operate this way? Here are their sources:

- Male colleagues at work, who are veterans of the American Dog House and who think they are viable models for all men everywhere.
- A guy you met in line at the grocery store, who told you his life story with women in five minutes, including his advice on how to handle women when the going gets tough.
- Your father, who never really told you how to avoid the American Dog House but thought he did.
- Your uncle on your father's side, who swore that he knew how to handle women and you could too if you would just take his advice.
- A taxi-cab driver in New York City, who told you that the way to get along with women and avoid the American Dog House is to lie.

No one, especially women, should be surprised when men paint themselves into a corner by parroting their male peers (young, old, or deceased). Men earn their entry into the American Dog House as a result of their own faults. They do not know how to avoid this fate. Will they ever learn? Who will teach them? Is it possible for men to reprogram themselves in a way that guarantees them safety from the American Dog House for more than twenty-four hours?

Getting into the American Dog House is easy. Getting out, however, is virtually impossible. And yet men know that women hold the key to their fate. Why not ask them to tell us how to get out? What have we got to lose?

Why Men Are Doomed

The men I know are fated to spend most of their waking hours in the American Dog House. Even if they deny this and try to argue against the inevitable, they will eventually discover the truth. Men are characteristically naive. Their naivete ensures their fate. This is so because men accept the erroneous advice of other men, who:

- Encourage them to ignore books, magazine articles, and other publications that are written to increase their sensitivity toward women.
- Tell them that it's cool to be macho and not to worry.
- Chide them for pandering to their wives or partners, calling them "pussy whipped" and subsequently causing them to alter their conduct and overall demeanor.
- Insist that "real men" display strength only when they stand their ground and refuse to give in.

Such advice conditions men in ways that eventually erode trust and seal their fate. In other words, men are doomed because, without thinking, they doom themselves by accepting the advice of other men who are equally doomed, which supports the idea that men are really ignorant. When men heed such advice, the following results are easy to predict:

1. Their wives or partners give them the "cold shoulder."
2. TV dinners suddenly increase, and home-cooked meals become obsolete.
3. New male friends of their wives or partners begin to appear.
4. Macho becomes the unutterable "M" word their wives or partners invoke.

It should not be difficult for most men to understand that they are actually the ones who create the conditions of their eventual demise. Men doom themselves to the American Dog House. They do not possess the wherewithal to extricate themselves from such an ungodly fate. In fact, they figure that their fate has been determined not because of their own conduct or actions, but because they are innocent victims of the women they profess to love. When this happens, here is what men do:

- They sulk like babies and seek comfort in sports bars or other places where men gather.
- They resort to name-calling and convince themselves that all women are bitches.
- They blame women rather than themselves for their fate.
- They call their mothers and tell them that the women they know are not like they were, but are blood-sucking members of NOW who have listened to too many Eleanor Smeal speeches.

What men do not understand when they do this is that such reactions only work to further seal their fates. Who knows how long these men will have to spend in the American Dog House? Men think they are more virtuous than they really are. There is a way out of this predicament. It's just a matter of time.

What Should Every Man Know?

There is, of course, no final answer to this question. Although men already know this, women think they have an inalienable right to tell the men they know what every man should know. Women are, however, mistaken to assume they know anything that would actually help their men. Only men know what's best. Here is what every man should know:

1. **Accept fate.** Do not argue with any woman who is on the verge of consigning you to the American Dog House. You will not win!
2. **Heed their advice.** Even if you think the advice women give you is transparent and full of holes, make believe you accept their rationale without question. This may mean the difference between one night in the American Dog House or what may seem like an eternity.
3. **Women can be very vicious when they're upset.** They can also be very vicious when they are not upset. Just accept it. Do not try and dig your way out of the hole you have created by whining, promising to do better if she would only give you a second chance, or begging her

forgiveness. Such lame responses will only dig a deeper hole. They will also not alter your fate.

4. **Bite the bullet.** You'll get better over time if you can fake your regret. In other words, look as sad as you possibly can, visibly wipe away the tears you might be able to coax from one or both eyes, and say anything, even if it's out of desperation, from an all-fours position.

5. **The best way to a woman's heart is to repeat whatever she tells you to say.** Let her write your soliloquy, and then simply repeat it verbatim. Do not add any of your own words. Do not improvise. If she tells you to say, "I'm sorry," then just say it with meaning. If she assigns you more than one domestic task, ask her exactly when she would like these chores completed and begin work on her list of "honey dos" even before she stops talking. If she claims that you have never massaged her back, even though she has made repeated requests, find your way to the massage oil then and there, and offer to give her a back rub she will never forget.

If you can memorize what every man should know and call it up on demand, then perhaps the time you actually spend in the American Dog House for one or more infractions will be minimized. Isn't this worth the risk?

The Dog House Novice

Novices must enter the American Dog House alone. There are no exceptions to this rule. It is one of the rites of passage every young boy must experience. This usually happens during the adolescent years, between the ages of twelve and seventeen, when their girlfriends stop speaking to them after they commit their first major faux pas. This can be virtually anything. Your girlfriend might introduce you to the Dog House for any number of reasons, including these:

1. You were not where you told her you would be, and she found out.
2. A girlfriend of hers, otherwise known as an "informant," told her that she saw you with another girl at a local shopping mall.
3. You innocently forgot her birthday.
4. You said that you were scheduled to work when you knew that was a lie and you had plans to go out on the town with several of your young male friends.
5. You told your girlfriend that your mother wanted you to do a few chores around the house, and that you were not available.

Whenever any of these barefaced lies are discovered by the girl of your dreams, you are inaugurated into the Dog House for Adolescent Boys. This experience catches most boys by surprise, because they are novices and were never privy to the advice of their fathers or of older, more experienced men.

The novice is never prepared. He knows nothing about the real American Dog House. He thinks it's a place in his backyard where Rover lives. His ignorance is universal and can only be mitigated by real knowledge. This takes time. It also requires an older, more knowledgeable mentor, who can warn him in advance so that he can avoid such a fate. What young boys do not know and are too young to figure out for themselves is that older men are as naive as they are. That's why most of them spend a lot of time in the American Dog House. However, here is the advice savvy, older men like to give novices:

- Give your girlfriend a line about your ungodly and unmerciful parents, who constantly punish you by requiring you to complete all of the household chores on weekend nights.

- Find some guy you know to front for you by telling your girlfriend that you were with him and not with some other girl.
- Tell her that you really didn't forget her birthday, but that the surprise you had planned simply backfired.
- Tell her that you went out with the boys because one of them was suffering from depression, and that you and your friends were only trying to cheer him up.

If their advice does not work, then may I be the first to say, "Welcome to the American Dog House." As a Dog House novice, you have my best wishes!

Dog House 101: A Crash Course

Crash courses are dangerous for a number of reasons, especially for men. This is because the men who complete them think they're experts when they're not. Every introductory course, especially Dog House 101, should carry the following warning:

The completion of this course may not result in keeping you out of the American Dog House. It may also not influence your exit once you are in. Enroll at your own risk!

The development of course content is older than Adam. However, older does not necessarily mean better. This is especially applicable to the crash course called Dog House 101. In fact, this chapter is nothing more than my own meager attempt to provide a few suggestions for a more official and elaborate syllabus I may one day, in the not too distant future, publish.

Once academia gets wind of such a course, I expect to be contacted by any number of academic institutions and invited to submit a more official course description and syllabus for further consideration by catalog and curriculum committees everywhere.

Eventually, private or state universities and colleges would likely decide to offer it as a required college-level credit course of study only for male novices and veteran male students of the American Dog House. Wouldn't that be a welcome turn in the road for men everywhere? In the meantime, here are just a few important topics any Dog House 101 course should include:

1. **Never get married.** Doing this would be the equivalent of driving the last nail into your own coffin! Since all men are dogs, the decision to marry means that your wife would be given free reign to manage the leash she buckles around your neck anytime. Remaining single is your only viable option. Such a status does not include a leash. Never getting married assures you will never become a candidate for the American Dog House.

2. **Never buy a dog.** This means that you would never have to worry about the construction of an outdoor doghouse in which you, not your dog, would eventually reside. Avoid this dilemma at

any cost. Even if the dog you are tempted to buy is a miniature and ever so cute, don't do it! If you do, you will pay a price you will live to regret the rest of your married life.

3. **Talk with other men first.** This especially applies to those men you know who opted to marry against the better part of wisdom. They will tell you how to avoid a similar fate. Listen to their advice. They know. Their stories are an important part of the oral history of the American Dog House.

4. **Review comic-strip classics.** Find your way to your local newspaper and review at least the following two comic strip classics: *Blondie* and *Peanuts*. This may help you avoid the fate of Dagwood, the oldest living occupant of the American Dog House, or of Charlie Brown, who couldn't keep his foot out of his mouth if his life depended on it. Envision yourself as these infamous comic-strip characters. This may eventually work to your advantage.

5. **Watch *Everybody Loves Raymond* on television.** TV, in this case, may not be a waste

of your time. You may already know that Ray Barone, a successful sports columnist, is both over-mothered and over-wifed in virtually every episode of this hilarious and yet tragic sitcom. Not even Ray's father, Frank, or his brother, Robert, can free him from the Dog House in which he lands in almost every episode. Like Ray, Frank and Robert also reside in separate Dog Houses of their own making. A daily dose of this sitcom may deepen your commitment to avoid such a fate.

If you take the time to review the above unofficial syllabus for Dog House 101 and actually decide to enroll in the course and complete it successfully, you may be able to avoid the fate of other men who have never been introduced to such an intriguing academic option. If you succeed in this endeavor—and chances are that you will—you, too, may become a friend of the course, touting its virtues to every man you know. And, if this phenomenon occurs, they will be indebted to you forever! They may even kiss the ground on which you walk!

Another viable option is to review the following course outline details related to the above proposal. It's a hoot! It may even inspire you to enroll in this course on your way to becoming a real man.

DOG HOUSE 101
FOUR-YEAR DEGREE COURSE

Bachelor of Arts Degree

This is a new four-year degree now being offered at the undergraduate level. In just a matter of four academic semesters, you will become a model for all men everywhere, and earn your BA degreee in Male Studies to boot!

Please review the course outline details below, and then enroll in the course before you are sent headlong into the American Dog House again. Time is on your side, so don't hesitate! Enroll now!

FIRST SEMESTER
Fall Schedule:

DH 101:	Dogonomics
DH 102:	A Brief History of Male Superiority
DH 103:	Silence Does Not Give Consent
DH 104:	What Women Want

Spring Schedule:

DH 105:	Washing Your Own Clothes
DH 106:	Preparing Your Own Meals
DH 107:	Shopping at Your Own Risk
DH 108:	Respecting Her Property
DH 109:	The Discovery of Your Feminine Side

SECOND SEMESTER
Fall Schedule:

DH 201:	Behavior Therapy
DH 202:	Tragic Flaws You Own
DH 203:	Male Incompetence
DH 204:	Flowers Are Not Forever
DH 205:	Property Rights

Spring Schedule:

DH 206:	Sleep Deprivation
DH 207:	What to Do After the Sun Rises
DH 208:	What to Do After the Sun Sets
DH 209:	Taking Care of Your Own Junk

THIRD SEMESTER
Fall Schedule:

DH 301:	Male Innocence
DH 302:	Take the Bus and Leave the Driving to Her
DH 303:	Never Forget Special Days
DH 304:	Lip Service Does Not Work

Spring Schedule:

DH 305:	Fake What You Know
DH 306:	Don't Be Afraid to Ask for Help
DH 307:	Living without Sex I
DH 308:	Living without Sex II
DH 309:	Dog House Hell

FOURTH SEMESTER
Fall Schedule:

DH 401:	Kindness Kills
DH 402:	Say "Yes"
DH 403:	Learning How to Survive Loss

Spring Schedule:

DH 404:	The Plague of Mothers-in-Law
DH 405:	On Seeking the Advice of Men
DH 406:	Living on the Edge
DH 407	Listen, Pray, and Love

Prenuptial Agreements: Why Every Man Needs One

In order to avoid the fate and misery of the American Dog House, every man needs to write a prenuptial agreement with a "No Dog House" clause and require his wife-to-be to sign it on the day of his wedding, preferably in a dark room of the church, synagogue, or wedding chapel before the ceremony actually begins. If you wait until the cascading sound of the organ music begins or for the first soloist to belt out the Ave Maria, it will be too late. Your Best Man, in this case, might be very useful to you at this time, but only if the Maid of Honor is nowhere in sight. Your prenuptial agreement should read as follows:

Prenuptial Agreement

I, (insert the full name of your wife-to-be after you and your Best Man conduct an FBI search without questionable results), promise never to have a dog as a pet, since this would require the construction of a doghouse in our backyard under the guise that our dog, Spot, would actually reside there. Furthermore, I promise never to ask you to build

a gazebo and place it anywhere on our property, since this structure may be enclosed and considered by our family, friends, neighbors, and guests as a potential Dog House in which you, my future husband, may reside after one or more fights or arguments, none of which you would ever be able to win legally or otherwise.

_____

Signature/Wife-to-Be

_____

Witness/Best Man

This document, of course, is not legally binding, but it will disclose just how serious your wife-to-be really is about her impending marriage to you. If she really loves you as much as she says she does, then her willingness to sign such an agreement will be easy to secure. However, if she defaults and refuses to sign the agreement, may God Almighty have mercy on your soul! You may want to secure the services of a respected male attorney just in case this plan backfires and your fate as an American Dog House casualty is sealed.

Marriage Advice from a Dog House Veteran

In all my years of marriage, I have heard virtually nothing from anyone about how to forge a happy marriage. So I have taken it upon myself to advance a few suggestions of my own. I admit that I do not have the credentials of such marriage experts as Dr. Phil or Dr. Wayne Dyer. However, this deficiency may not disqualify me from at least trying to help other marriage novices figure out the best way to a happy marriage. Here is my advice:

1. **Listen to your wife.** Listening is a learned art. I should know. As a professor, I can tell when my students are truly engaged. I can also tell when they are not listening. As my wife's husband-for-life, I am as guilty as many of my married male counterparts of this mortal sin. My wife knows this, too. She also knows when I tune her out. This bad habit will not lead to a happy marriage. My wife has the uncanny ability to tell me what I do not want to hear about myself. I will admit that it is difficult to listen to anyone who loves you tell you the truth about yourself, but such medicine is good for the soul. It may even help

you to see your flaws in a more objective way. Anyone can benefit from this.

2. **Stop complaining about the past.** Since nobody really cares about your sordid regrets, you shouldn't either. Put the past behind you! Put a match to your pile of regrets—the lost loves you may have experienced, the estranged friends, the botched education, the unwritten novel, the failed investments, the dear friend who committed suicide, the opportunities that sailed away without you, your dysfunctional family—and just let them blow away. Instead, find something in the here-and-now that truly absorbs you and take up with that. You will eventually discover that releasing the past will free your marriage and make it possible for you to experience true happiness.

3. **Recognize the value of interdependence.** Teamwork is not only a value shared by the corporate world. It is also the essence of a happy marriage. Let's face it: My wife possesses admirable qualities. She is articulate, knows how to save money, is family-oriented, enjoys good

times with friends, and is a seasoned extrovert. I am, on the other hand, her opposite. To me, it is essentially our inequality that will make our marriage a happy experience for both of us.

This is what makes the tapestry of marriage beautiful in its own right. My advice is only a first step in the journey of love called marriage. There is more work to do!

Is There A Dog House For Women?

Obviously not!

Sex in the American Dog House

If you are a male over fifty, you can forget about sex if you have been consigned to the American Dog House by your wife or partner. Had this happened when you were in your midtwenties or slightly older, you would have stood a better chance. But now that you are over fifty, even the thought of having sex during your confinement in the American Dog House is nothing more than a pipe dream. This is primarily because men over fifty do not know how to beg for what they want. They are, more often than not, too proud to see that even the appearance of humility may yield the results they seek.

Men should blame their fathers, who swore by the Principle of Patriarchy. Men of your father's generation avoided any expression of humility as a sign of weakness. Think about what these men could have gained had they been able to suppress their pride. Since this was not possible at that time, all men today suffer from a similar condition. The way out of this conundrum is for men to return to the lost art of begging for sex. You, too, can adopt these rules. Here they are:

The Rules of Begging

1. **Ask for what you want in a surreptitious way.** Women communicate indirectly. They always have. This may require you to say things like, "Honey, I've been in the Dog House now for less than twenty-four hours, and I'm *so* lonely without you." Remember to exaggerate the word "so." You may discover that this first rule of begging will yield the first crack in the tightly bolted door of your own Dog House.

2. **Try faking bodily injury.** Most women I know will cave in when the man in their life is hurting. Women are simply built this way. They are nurturers. Your task, then, is to play on their sympathy. That's the other, more respectful word to remember. You can do this by faking bodily injury. Just tell your wife or partner that the hard dirt floor of your Dog House has wrenched your back or lower spine, and you can barely move. Such a physical condition, even if it's fake, may prompt the one you love to give you a back rub you will never forget. Once the

back rub is over, remember to tell her that you are already feeling a lot better and that your pain is already beginning to subside. Faking bodily injury may lead to a second crack in the tightly bolted door of your own Dog House, and ultimately to sex.

3. **An honest confession is good for the soul.** This rule has been historically touted by the religious community as one of its virtues. Just tell your wife or partner that you have begged God Almighty to forgive you for the offenses you have committed, and that you, with the help of God himself, vow never to repeat the sins which got you into this mess in the first place.

This third and final rule of begging is better known as "lying." Lying is a male art. Since most women I know are empathetic, they will accept your confession as genuine and grant you the benefit of the doubt. Such a confession of guilt on your part may soften the woman you love and prompt her to either forgive you outright or to at least forgive you but never, ever forget.

Her actual response to your confession does not matter. What matters is that it may lead to the third and final crack in the tightly bolted door of your own Dog House. Count your lucky stars if this happens. The sex you crave is now just minutes away. If what I have suggested fails, then perhaps you might want to kiss sex in the American Dog House good-bye for now and consider monastic life as a possible new career.

Dog House Economics

Most men are particularly vulnerable when it comes to money. This is especially true if a joint bank account is maintained and paying bills together with your wife or partner is a collaborative exercise. However, once you as a man are cast into the fiery pit of the American Dog House, everything on the economic front will change unless you had the foresight to open your own checking and savings accounts, which I strongly advise. This outcome is inevitable. It is also not subject to negotiation. Once the dastardly deed is done and your confinement begins, a realistic budget must be defined. This will require considerable reflection on your part. It also assumes that your income will be unavailable to meet your expenses, especially because your wife or partner will need every last dime of yours to maintain your primary residence even though, at least temporarily, you would be unsure about the length of time you would actually remain in the American Dog House.

You do not have to be a Certified Public Accountant to either create your first Dog House budget or maintain it. Also, do not count on tax breaks once April 15 of your first year of occupancy rolls around. There are none! Your only obligation is to create a realistic budget and to live within your means.

I have discovered that a monthly budget is by far the more viable route based on occupancy rates, which rarely exceed one month. You may be able to gain the advantage of what the Irish call "the luck of the draw" if you pay careful attention to the advice I have already provided and demonstrate a commitment to implement what you have already learned. All of this may shorten your stay as a "first timer" or even as a veteran of the American Dog House. However, don't count on it. Your occupancy may last longer than3 you think. Here is my proposed thirty-day American Dog House budget:

- **Rent/$800**: This amount is the equivalent of your average furnished efficiency apartment. It is the most basic of all available options.

- **Electricity/$35**: The only expenditure on this line of your monthly budget is for the rotating ceiling fan you may want to install in your temporary quarters. Air-conditioning is out of the question, especially given the total number of square feet available. If you opted to install even the smallest AC unit available in today's market, you would most likely freeze your ass off. Climatic conditions would make you feel as if you were living in a supermarket freezer. Use only a ceiling fan. It's not only cheaper, but it will also circulate the air enough to reduce your chances of heat exhaustion. Your health is more important than your comfort.

- **Blankets (two only)/$24.95**: Blankets are absolutely necessary, especially if your occupancy either begins or extends into the winter months. Of course, this really depends on your geographic location. I pity you if you live north of the Mason-Dixon Line or somewhere out west. Florida, or any other similar location, is preferable because of its tropical climate. Beggars, however, can't be choosers, so just make the best of your American Dog House experience regardless of where you actually reside or what the temperature is. That's why I have proposed that you purchase two blankets and two blankets only. Make sure that one blanket is lightweight enough for moderate to hot and humid evenings. Your second blanket should be a lot heavier, especially if you live up north, which is frequently buried under feet of snow in the dead of winter. You will eventually thank me for my two-blanket proposal.

- **Food/$1,000**: Since your wife or partner will not be preparing dinner or any other meal for you during your stint in the American Dog House, the only two options available to you are to dine out or use available takeout services at specified restaurants located as close as possible to your temporary abode. You will discover that both options are more expensive than you ever imagined. Get used to it. However, since I, along with other male friends of mine, frequent a local Waffle House in Orlando, Florida, I would highly recommend that you purchase your meals on a takeout basis at a Waffle House of your own choosing or its equivalent located as close as possible to your new residence.

- **Water and other miscellaneous services/$0**: This will cost you absolutely nothing, as you will be using the lawn and garden hose of your home in which your wife or partner now resides without you. You will, of course, need to drink plenty of water daily, as this will prevent dehydration. Also, locate at least one or two massive bushes as close as possible to your new residence that would serve your urinary and defecation needs. Trees, in this case, have also functioned as a man's best friend. Use them. You have no other option. After all, dogs don't need bathroom facilities!

This proposed thirty-day budget can be adjusted on an "as needed" basis. You will discover that the economic restraints under which you must now live will eventually be lifted only if your wife or partner permits your return home. In the meantime, don't sweat the small stuff. Just do your best with what you have. You will survive.

The Waffle House: A Dog's Best Friend

I have been a regular customer of a Waffle House in Orlando, Florida, for almost twenty years now. It's a stone's throw from one of the state's twenty-eight community colleges where I teach in the Department of Fine Arts as a professor of humanities. As part of my routine, I stop for coffee there at 5:00 AM every weekday morning and return again for coffee at four PM. Since every man needs a cave, I have adopted the Waffle House as my "malc cave." So have several other male friends of mine I have come to know over the years. Although we refer to one another fondly as "bums," we are more often known as "dogs." Even the waiters and waitresses who serve us daily know this about us. They are also privy to the zesty dialogue that occurs between us each day. Our focus is usually on such debatable issues as politics, economics, same-sex relationships, war, gas prices, immigration, and, of course, marriage.

We are all lost souls, or what you might call the Waffle House equivalent of the ten little Indians. Most of us are married. The rest are not much better off despite their single status. We all have issues, and our relationships with the opposite sex vary. Only two women we know are also regular customers. They know us better than we know ourselves. They also know that we are all dogs who have formed a brotherhood of sorts among the like-minded. What other option do we really have? Despite these variables, we have become experts in dispensing advice to one another, and even to other male guests we don't even know. Here is a sample of our advice on marriage, relationships, and the American Dog House:

1. **Every true marriage or relationship requires a Dog House.** Our wives and even the girlfriends of several male friends of ours already know this. Our experience supports this conclusion. None of us can claim exemption on this count. All of us have spent at least one or more lonely and sleepless nights in the American Dog House. As survivors, we have lived to tell our own unique stories to anyone who will listen. Marriage without a Dog House is a virtual impossibility!

2. **All men are dogs.** This conclusion is the result of a unanimous consensus among us. It is not

the result of coercion. We freely admit this, even though such an admission is painful. Over coffee, as I have already said, we even refer to each other as "dogs." Such a label has been etched into our souls. It's tattoolike.

3. **Every man needs a cave.** Unfortunately, male caves are very hard to find. According to available data, there are more women than men in the world these days. This means that women, with the exception of the two we know who frequent the Waffle House, can be found in almost every other public establishment, like spas, health-food restaurants, and nail salons. This is why we have adopted the Waffle House as our male cave.

Alas, we men are in the majority at the Waffle House. We sit together in virtually the same area every day without the interference of women. Every man needs a cave, especially when most of our waking hours each day are spent away from home. We already know that a home-based cave of a different kind awaits us. The Waffle House, however, is our self-chosen, away-from-home American Dog House. Although we know where the original one is, we prefer this one. After all, the Waffle House *is* a dog's best friend!

is There a Global Dog House?

Although the Dog House is an original American phenomenon, dating to before our country declared its independence in 1776, my research shows that it also exists internationally. In fact, virtually every country in the civilized and not-so-civilized world has its own version of the American Dog House in place. Below are several global versions of the American Dog House. The eyewitness accounts I have collected as a form of oral history support this conclusion. I have intentionally decided not to tamper with these accounts, but to permit them to speak on their own. The unique form the American Dog House has taken in each of the countries referenced below is obvious. Here are their stories:

The Mexican Dog House

Although you might think that the advent of Chipotle as the newest Mexican grill in town or the obvious success of Taco Bell over the years may soften your view of Mexican men, think again. Why do you really think the issue of immigration into the United States across the Mexican border has become such a monumental problem in recent years? It's because Mexican men are taking more of an initiative to escape, once and for all, from the tight grip their women have always had on them. Mexican men are actually docile creatures. They are all very humane and caring individuals. Since such qualities have never been appreciated by Mexican women, Mexican men have decided to cross the border illegally in pursuit of greater freedom.

The mystique of *abuela* or the Mexican version of "grandmother" still haunts Mexican men in all parts of that country. Why do you think Mexico City has been gradually sinking below sea level for decades now? It's because of the dead weight of this tradition on the backs of Mexican men. Whatever *Abuela* wants, *Abuela* gets! Mexican men are only the innocent victims of the shenanigans their women have orchestrated. They have done virtually nothing to deserve this fate. This is why the Mexican Dog House is virtually vacant today.

The Italian Dog House

Mamma Mia! Have you ever wondered about the history of this unique and often repeated Italian phrase? Its history is based on male exasperation. Italian men have never been able to please their mothers! Is it any wonder, then, that they have also never been able to please their wives, girlfriends, aunts, grandmothers, partners, or lovers? Since Italian men have always disappointed their women, they have turned to soccer as a way out of this dilemma. Why do you think Italy won the World Cup in soccer in 2006?

Since soccer is a male-dominated sport, it offers Italian men a viable way out of the Italian Dog House. Italian men are very sensitive and loving creatures. They cry at the drop of a hat. Since this has never been truly understood by Italian women, especially by their mothers, wives, girlfriends, aunts, grandmothers, partners, or lovers, soccer has historically provided Italian men with an easy way out of the Italian Dog House. Why accept confinement when you can gain the release afforded by the agile sport of soccer? The only other option available to Italian men is to become active in the Mafia. Such a choice, however, is much too dangerous to pursue. Soccer is the safer route. At least you may gain the benefit of a trophy and international recognition if you and your team become World Cup Champions!

The Chinese Dog House

Chinese men have always had an obvious advantage. This has always been the case. Unlike other men, Chinese men have always been able to have their cake and eat it, too. Otherwise, how would you explain the concept of the "little wife," which is so well-known in China and in other parts of Asia? This idea applies equally to both single and married Chinese men. These men have prerogatives no other man in the civilized world has ever experienced. Let's call such men "Asian Polygamists."

Chinese men may, in fact, be very married, but their monogamy is fictional. In other words, they have the best of all possible worlds. Their primary or "main wife" may be "supplemented," for want of a better word, with a "little wife." This is why Chinese men, even when they are sent to their version of the American Dog House, are in a win-win situation. The Chinese Dog House is always occupied by more than one "little wife." This must mean that infidelity is not really a punishable offense. Aren't Chinese men lucky?

After your review of the above eyewitness accounts, you might be tempted to create your own hybrid of the diverse forms the Dog House has taken in other countries around the world. This may work to your advantage, but I wouldn't bet on it. A Dog House is a Dog House is a Dog House. If all men are dogs, does it really matter where you live in the world? Besides, the so-called stories or eyewitness accounts I provided are really my own creations. I interviewed no one. This must mean that I am still a dog like other international friends of mine on whose experiences these fictional accounts are based. Gotcha!

Myths and Misconceptions Women Believe about Men: Are All Men Dogs?

The answer to the question this chapter raises is a resounding "yes"! All men are dogs! This is a view most men I know hold of themselves. It is also a view held by most women. How important is it to list a few of the myths and misconceptions about men first, which the women I know have embraced over the years? My intention, of course, is not to convince you, if you're a woman, to abandon such myths or misconceptions, but only to reinforce their accuracy. This may take most of the weight off of me and other men I know. This will free us to fulfill the biases women already have against us. Since we can do nothing to change their minds, we might as well just own up to their view of us. Here are the major myths and misconceptions women believe about men:

1. **All men are insensitive.** Say what you will about this myth, but the men I know will concede as much. They will say that their feelings, for good or ill, come first! This, of course, adds ammunition to the loaded and cocked gun women hold against the head of their men. There is no extrication from this fate. Men

doom themselves to the American Dog House. Their insensitivity has sent them there!

2. **All men resist change.** In fact, they abhor it! Women already know this about men. That's why the men they know are transparent. Women view the changes men say they are willing to make as conditional and fake.

3. **All men are blind.** Like the Cyclops of Greek fame, men see things only with one eye. Their vision is severely limited. They do not see things beyond the literal plane whenever women tell them how blind they really are. There is always a double meaning in what men say. This male weakness prompts women to send men into the American Dog House without passing "go."

4. **All men are deaf.** Men suffer as much from this impairment as they do from other illnesses. They cannot fake what they say they've never heard when women tell them what poor listeners they really are. Attempts by women to inspire men to develop more effective listening skills fall on deaf ears. This weakness usually leads to yet another episode of Dog House confinement.

These myths and misconceptions only provoke men to become more defensive. Such a response only reinforces their accuracy. Women know us better than we know ourselves. To them, we are nothing more than insensitive, resistant, blind, and deaf! That's precisely why women are convinced that all men *are* dogs!

Tips from a Dog House Veteran

I could say that I don't ever remember being consigned to the American Dog House, but that would be nothing more than a barefaced lie. At my age now, I could also tell you that my Dog House memories are fading, but that would also qualify as another barefaced lie. The fact is that I vividly remember every detail as a survivor of the American Dog House. I hope that you will learn as much as you possibly can from me so that you might be able to avoid a similar fate.

My Dog House memories are intact. They actually began over forty years ago. I am, therefore, a seasoned Dog House veteran. This is why you should glean as much as you possibly can from what I am about to tell you.

Tip #1: My hard exterior has probably been one of the primary factors in every American Dog House confinement I have ever experienced over the years. I am, by most estimates, a hard-ass! This means that what rolls off my tongue is infrequently filtered until it's too late and the damage has already been done. My recovery from this fate and return to "normalcy," whatever that means, eventually happens, but the time I have spent in the American Dog House far exceeds the time I have spent out of it. Any man worth his salt could learn a lot from me on this count. Find a way to lower your guard, permit your "softer self" to surface, and keep your damn mouth shut until you can say whatever you want to say in a much less volatile way.

Tip #2: I am also so set in my ways that I seldom show obvious signs that I am more than willing to revise the view I hold about virtually anything. This is a form of male dogmatism I share with many other men I know. Holding my ground in this way has made effective communication between me and my wife almost impossible to achieve, except on rare occasions. This form of male fanaticism has prompted my spouse to send me, more than once, headlong into the American Dog House for longer than I care to remember. In order to avoid a similar fate, show your wife or partner that the views you hold are not written in concrete, and that you are flexible enough to revise them in ways that are much less dogmatic. Doing this will speak volumes, and it may lessen the frequency of your American Dog House "visits."

Tip #3: Finally, find genuine ways to compliment your wife or partner so that her responses to your periodic displays of stupidity will be much less reactive. It is very easy for us, as men, to slip foolishly into a routine. I should know. Break your inane routines and consider one of the following options: (1) Be spontaneous. Not everything you do must conform to a rigid, preplanned schedule. (2) Buy flowers or anything else you know your wife or partner might really appreciate, and present your gift to her when there is nothing special to celebrate. Women accept such gestures as totally unrehearsed. It catches them by surprise. (3) Plan overnight trips together at times to a destination neither of you has ever experienced. This may awaken a side of her that may knock your socks off!

You have my legal permission to use these tips as part of your own game plan. I can do a lot better than I have in the past! So can you! If we, as men, are successful at implementing what I have suggested above, our visits to the American Dog House may be less frequent than we have ever experienced.

How to Get Out

Women hold the key to your exit from the American Dog House. However, getting out may be nothing more than an exercise in futility unless you pay close attention to the suggestions I'm about to give you. Although these suggestions may not expedite your exit, they may give you enough hope so that faith in yourself and in other men you know may be restored. Here is what may eventually free you from the involuntary confinement you have experienced in the past:

1. **Breaking out is not an option!** As you already know, most prisoners who are successful enough to orchestrate a jail or prison break are eventually captured and returned to solitary confinement. This is a worse condition. A better option is for you to accept your sentence, and hope for an early release.

2. **Cooperation is essential.** Find it in yourself to give your unqualified consent to the conditions of your confinement, and fulfill its terms without bitching. Your wife or partner may then decide to grant you a reprieve or to reduce your

sentence. You already know that teamwork, within the corporate context, is rewarded. Why would you doubt that cooperation, even under the conditions you often face, would not be equally rewarded?

3. **Beg frequently.** Begging is not a sign of male weakness. Look as sad as you possibly can, shed a tear or two so as to reinforce the depth and degree of the pain and suffering you have endured, and call out your honey's name more than once in the dead of night when she can hear you over the din of traffic and your loud neighbors and their children. Women love begging!

4. **Retain the "all fours" position at all costs.** Standing upright in front of the American Dog House never works. This posture only conveys defiance. Anytime you enter or exit the Dog House, do it in the "all fours" position. This will convince your wife or partner that you are truly sorry for the misery you have caused her. This posture of regret may help facilitate your exit.

I wish you only the very best in your attempts to resolve the dilemma you have created. If what I have suggested above does not work, do not call me! I will be much too busy trying hard to avoid reentering the American Dog House.

Epilogue
The American Dog House and the Future

Since we are almost at the end of the first decade of the twenty-first century, we should all know by now that the American Dog House is here to stay. It is alive and well. It is also a permanent part of the fabric of what makes us Americans. Its future is not a topic of debate. Here is what you can expect in the decades ahead:

All women, regardless of their age, will form and maintain circles of collaboration that will guarantee the survival of the American Dog House. Since women like to talk about men behind their backs, they will continue to orchestrate their own irreversible plot to keep Dog House restraints on men. As effective communicators, women will also transmit their knowledge about men to their own daughters, as well as to other women they know. Men will never be able to win this war and should surrender now!

No matter what men do, as individuals or as part of a group, they will never be able to gain exemption as Dog House candidates. Every dog has his day. Since all men are dogs, this applies to them as well. This truism is written in concrete. It is irreversible. All women agree that exemptions are illegal maneuvers orchestrated by men to gain their freedom from the American Dog House, once and for all, but they will not succeed.

Talk is cheap, and it always will be. Men have been conditioned by their fathers and by other men to employ talk as their method of emancipation. They have been told that they can talk their way out of a paper bag if they can only find the right words. Try as they will, this will not work now or in the decades ahead. Women already know this. They know that all men use flowery language as a last resort. Women will continue to embrace the view that talk is cheap.

Finally, there are no better days ahead for the American Dog House. It will always be nothing more than a rundown, unpainted hovel of a place constructed of boards and nails, with a dirt floor, no electricity, and your own dog dish placed on the ground just outside of its open door. Welcome home!